Coloring Books For Boys

Coloring Pages for Kids

By Gala Publication

PUBLISHED BY:

Gala Publication

ISBN-13: 978- 1508815884
ISBN-10: 1508815887

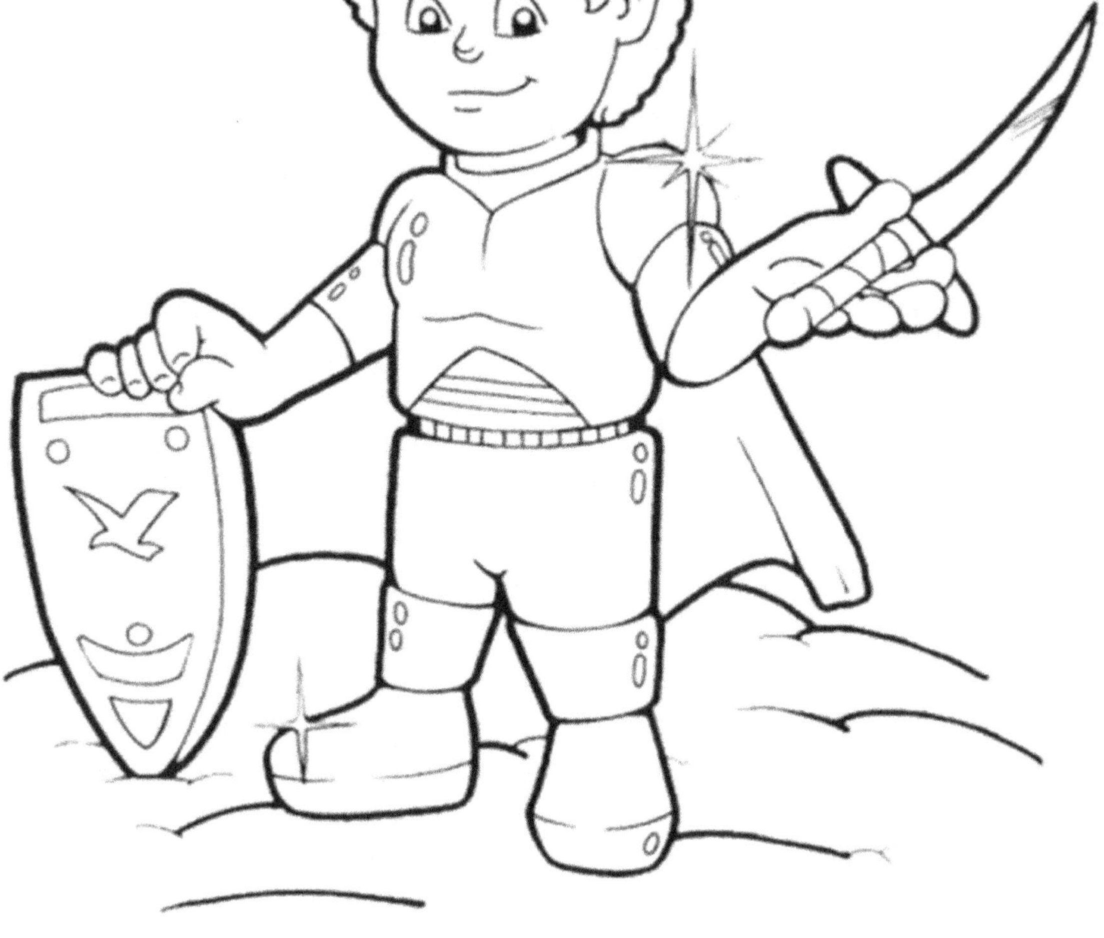

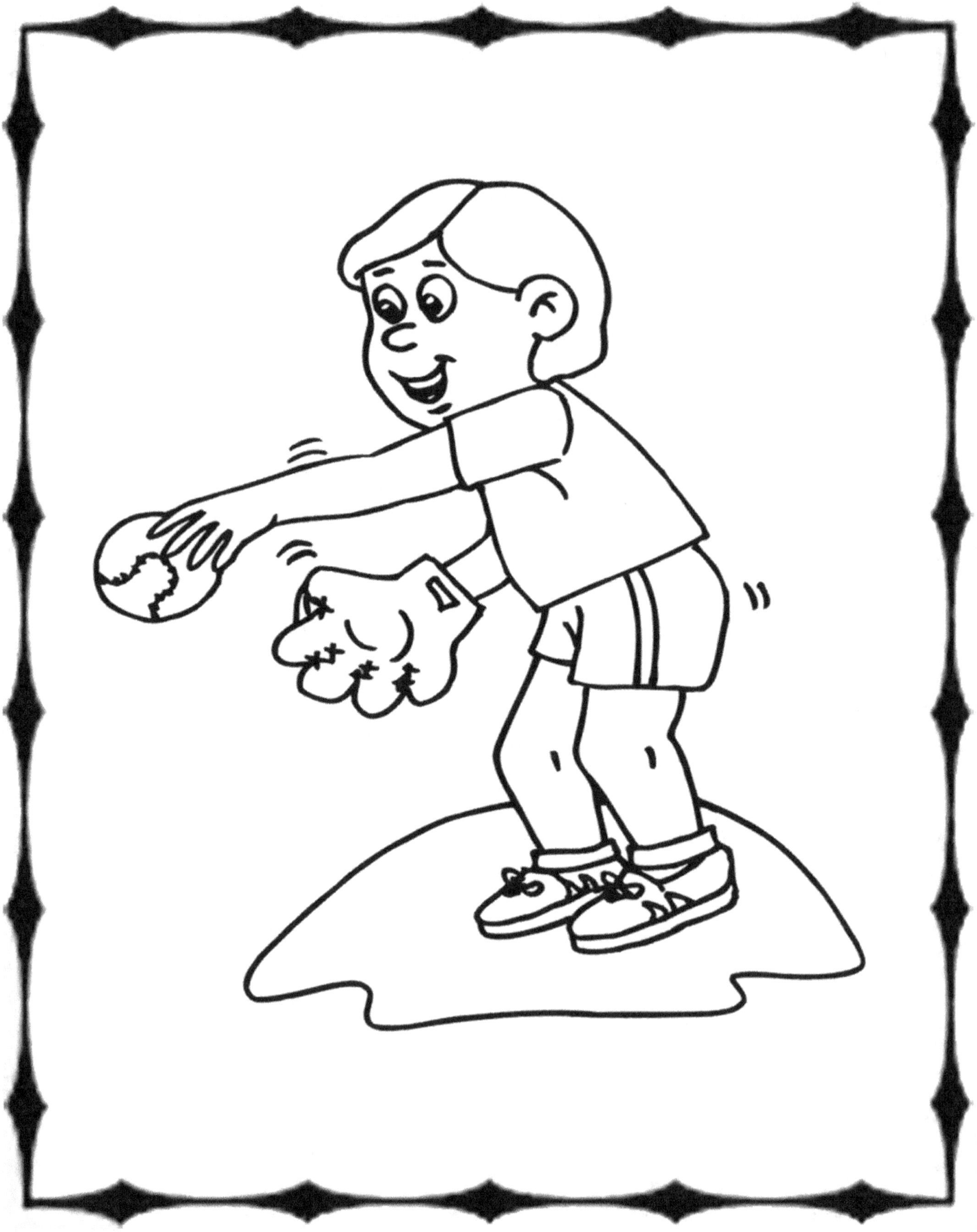

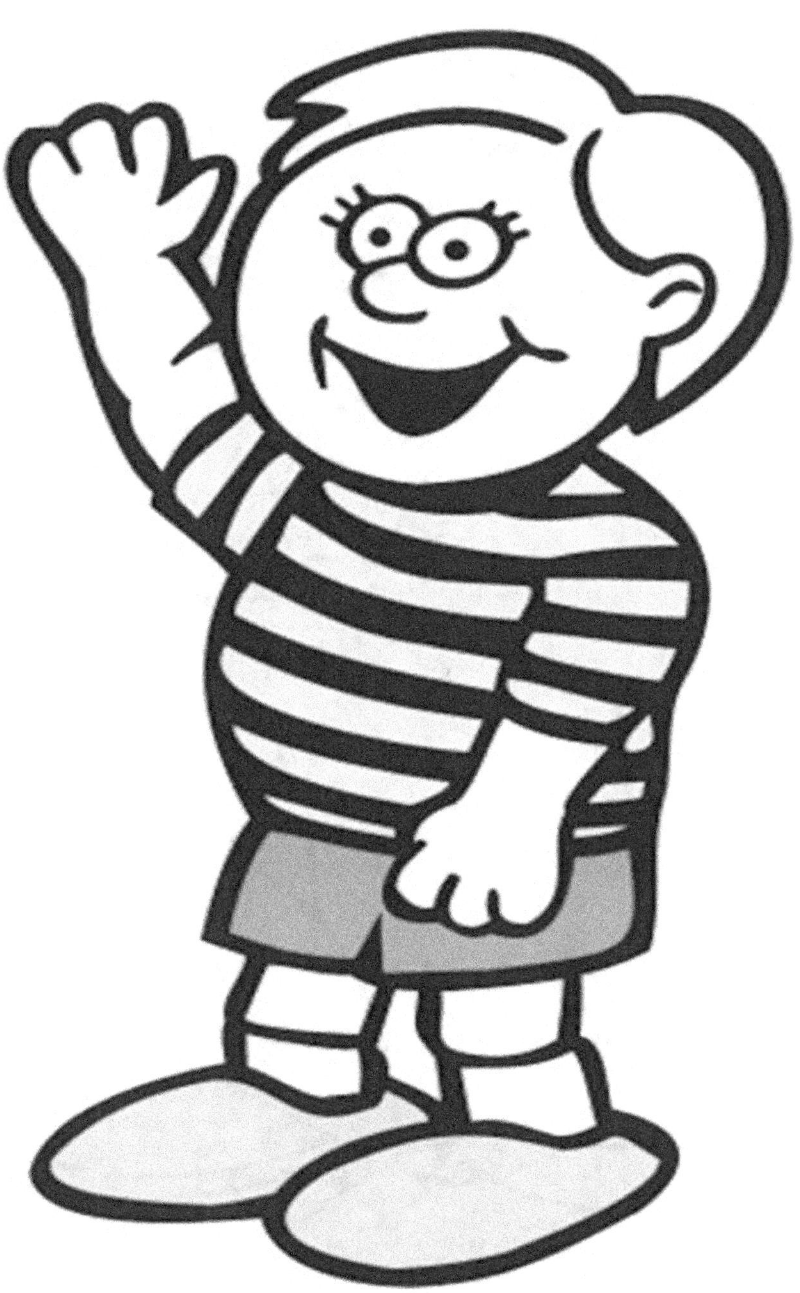

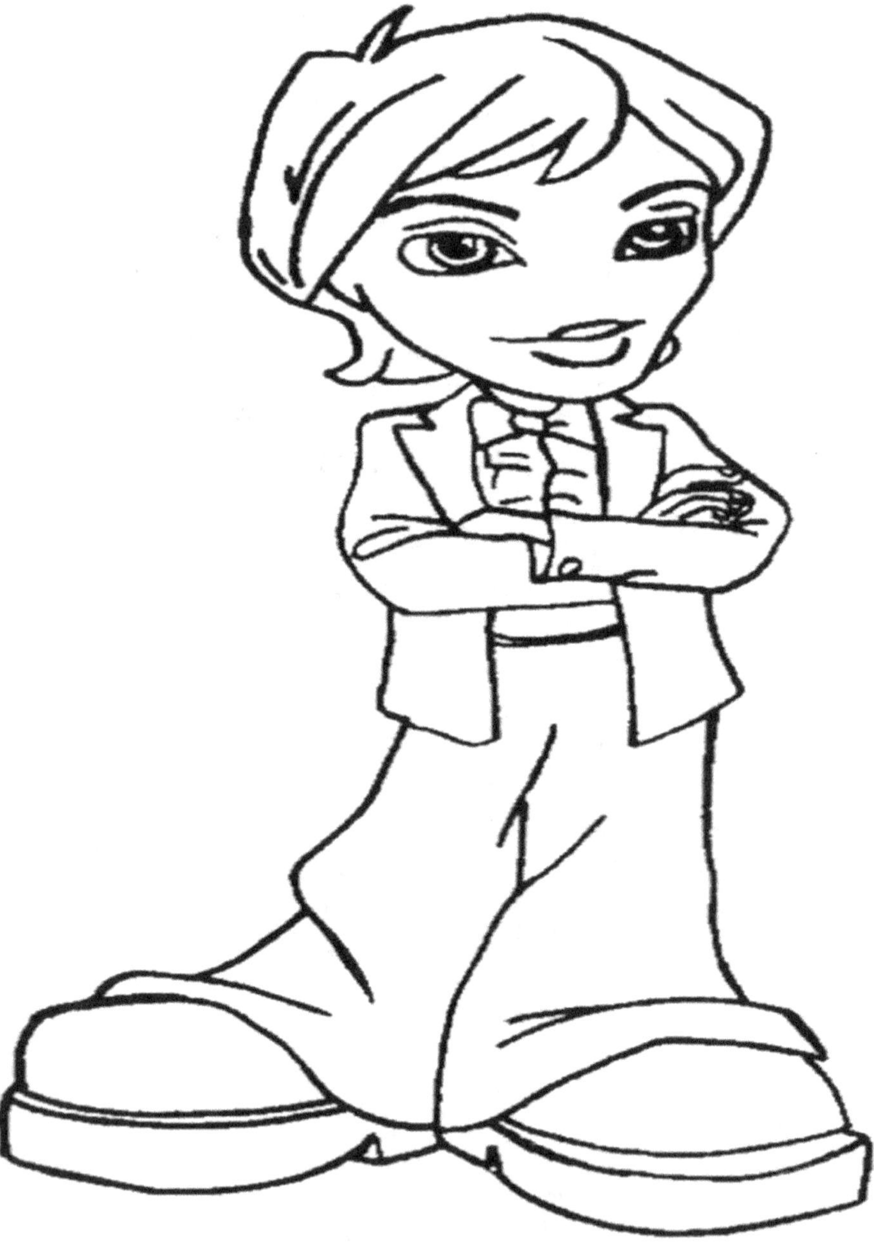

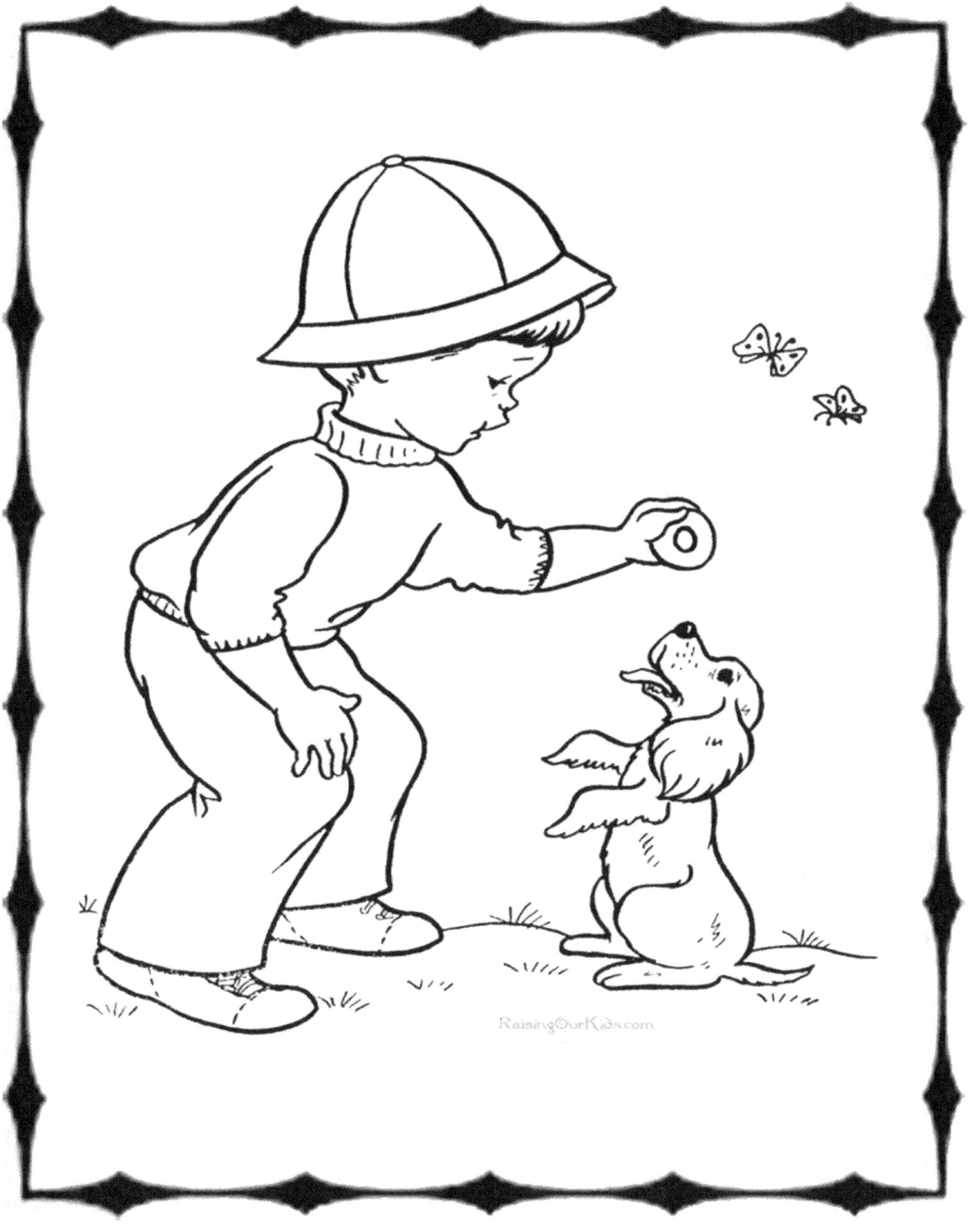
RaisingOurKids.com

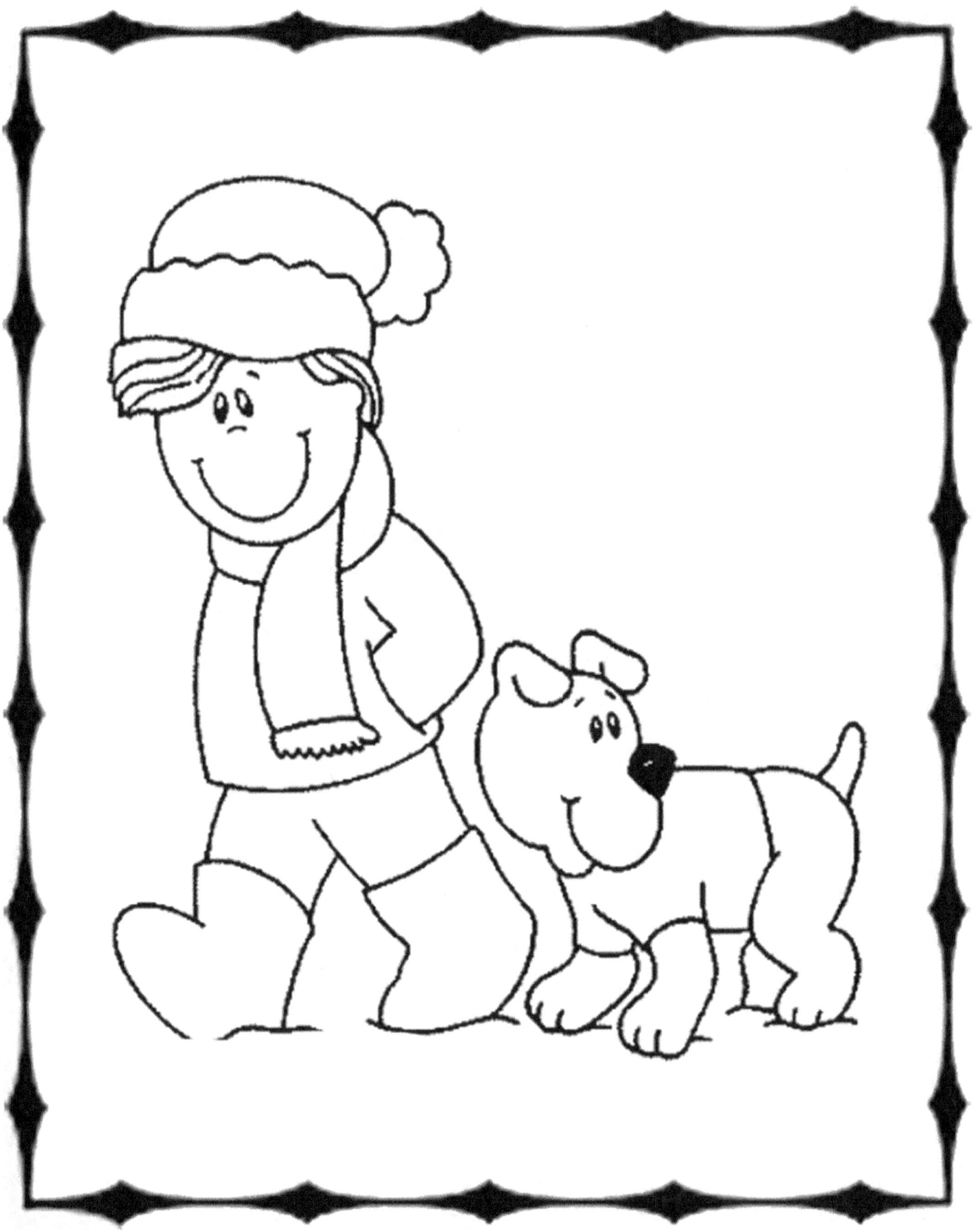

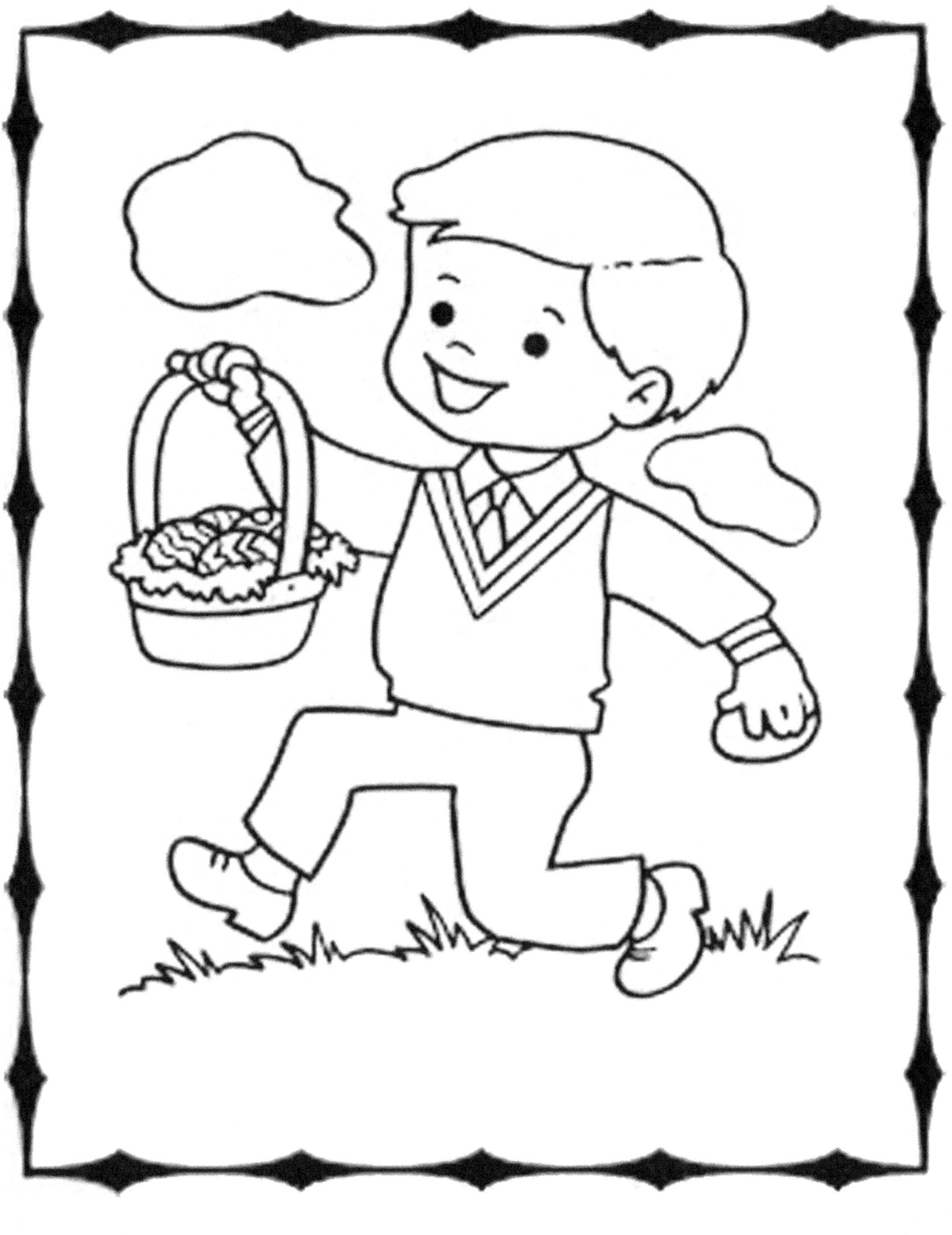

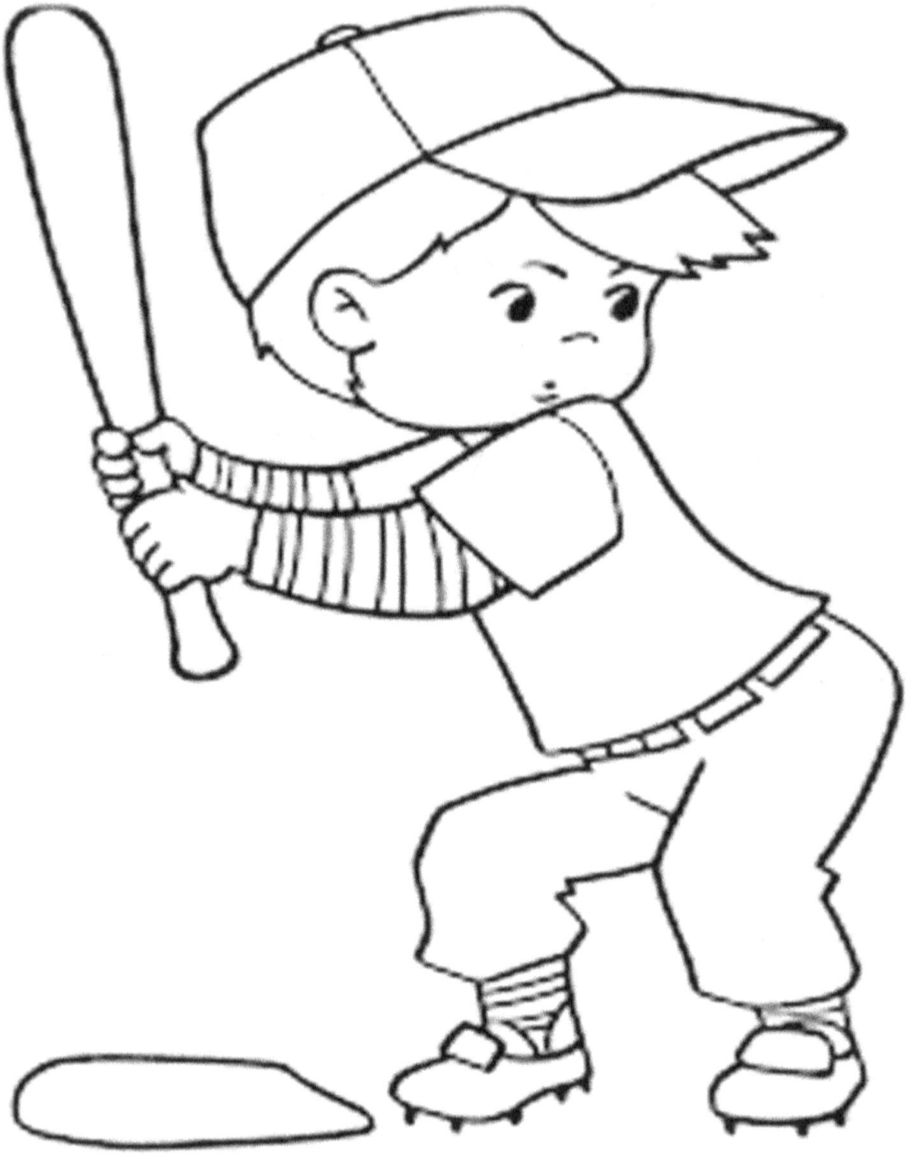

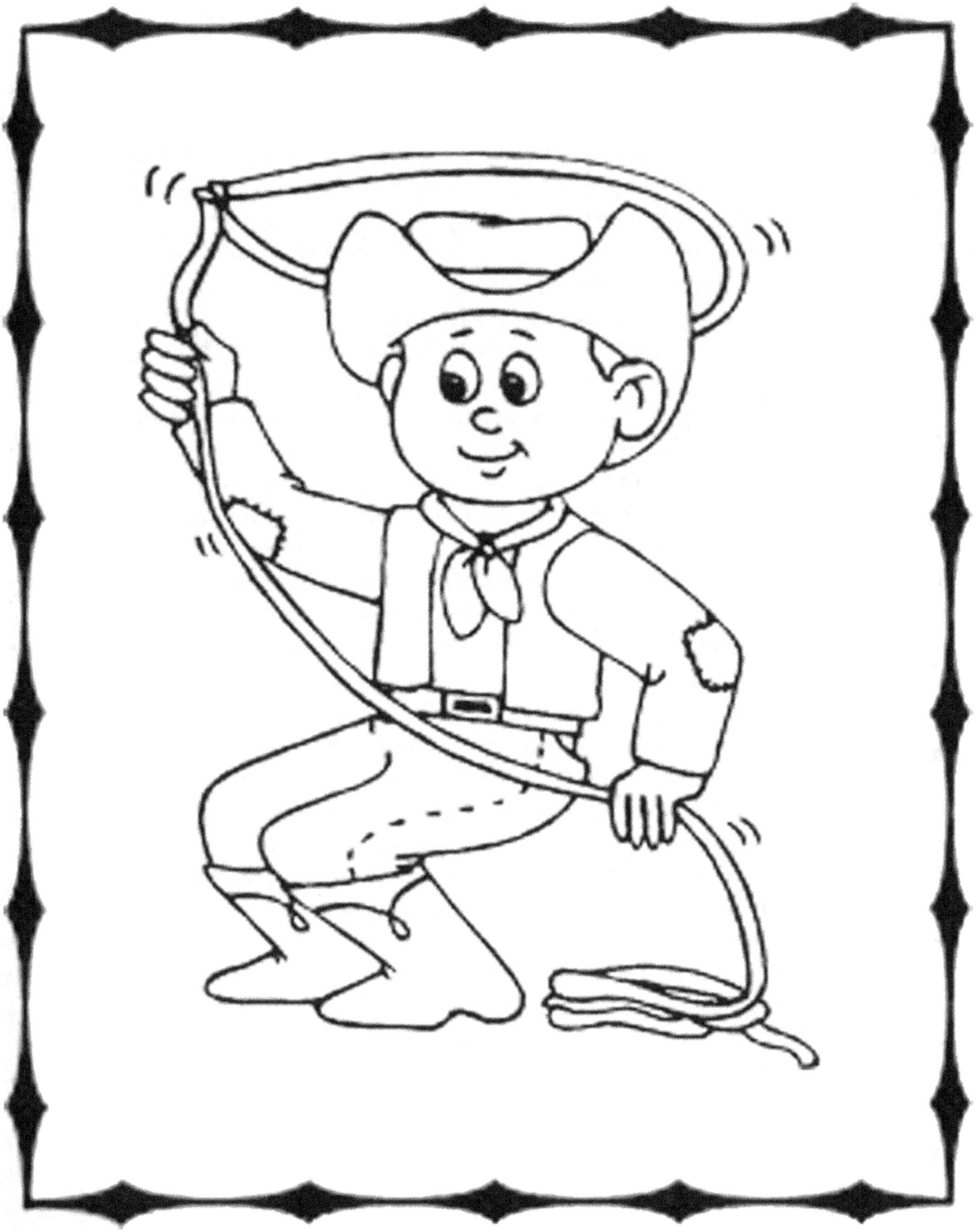

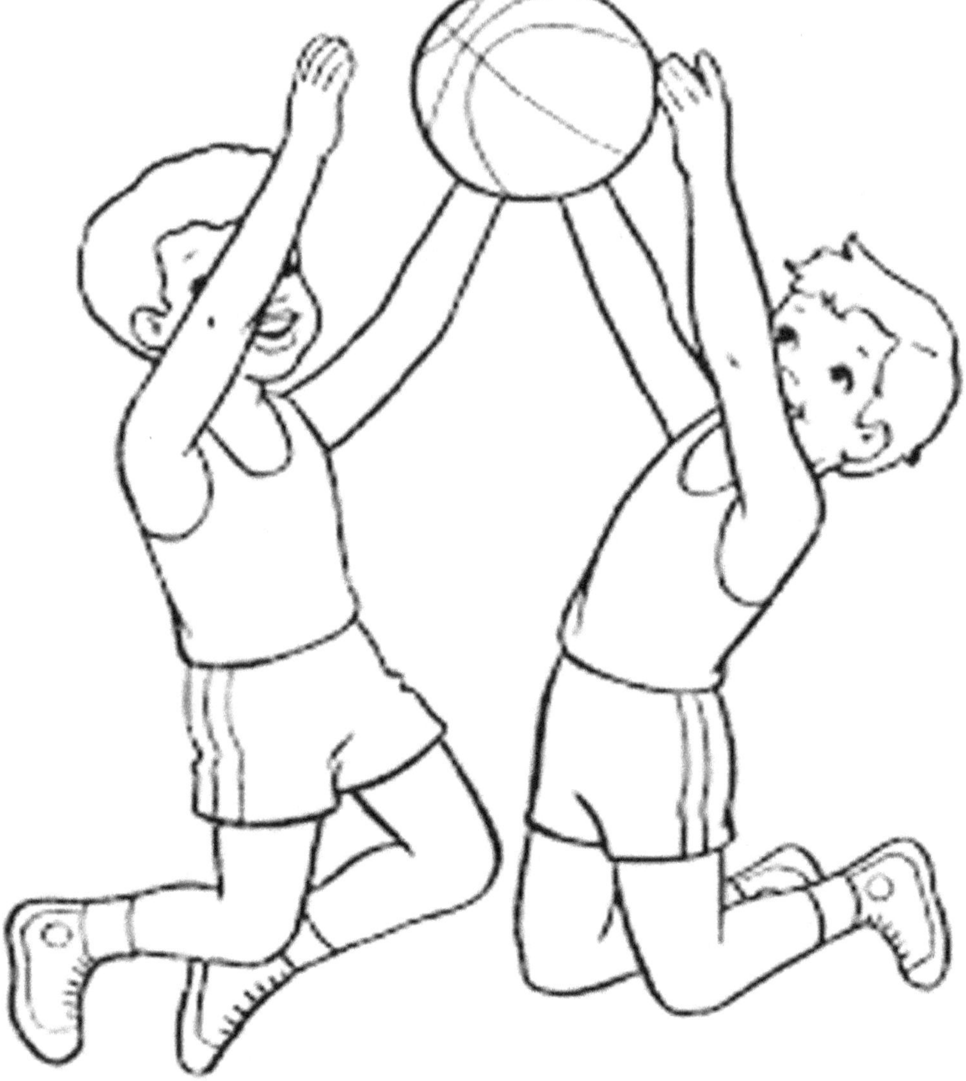

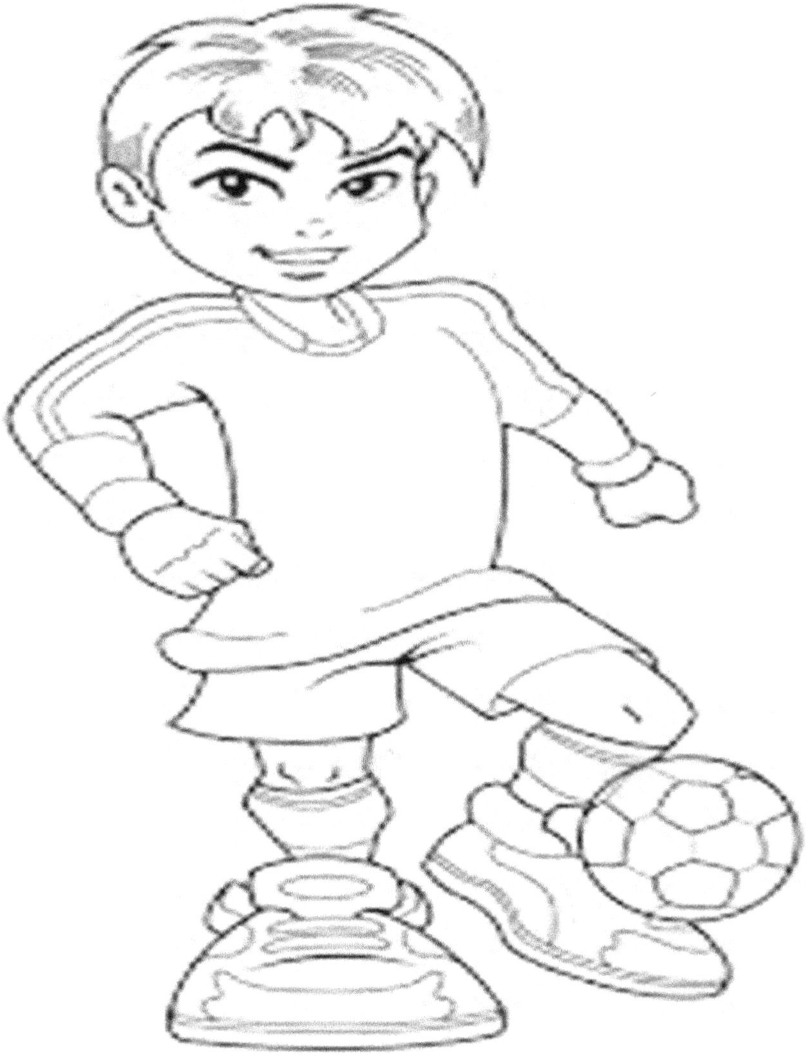

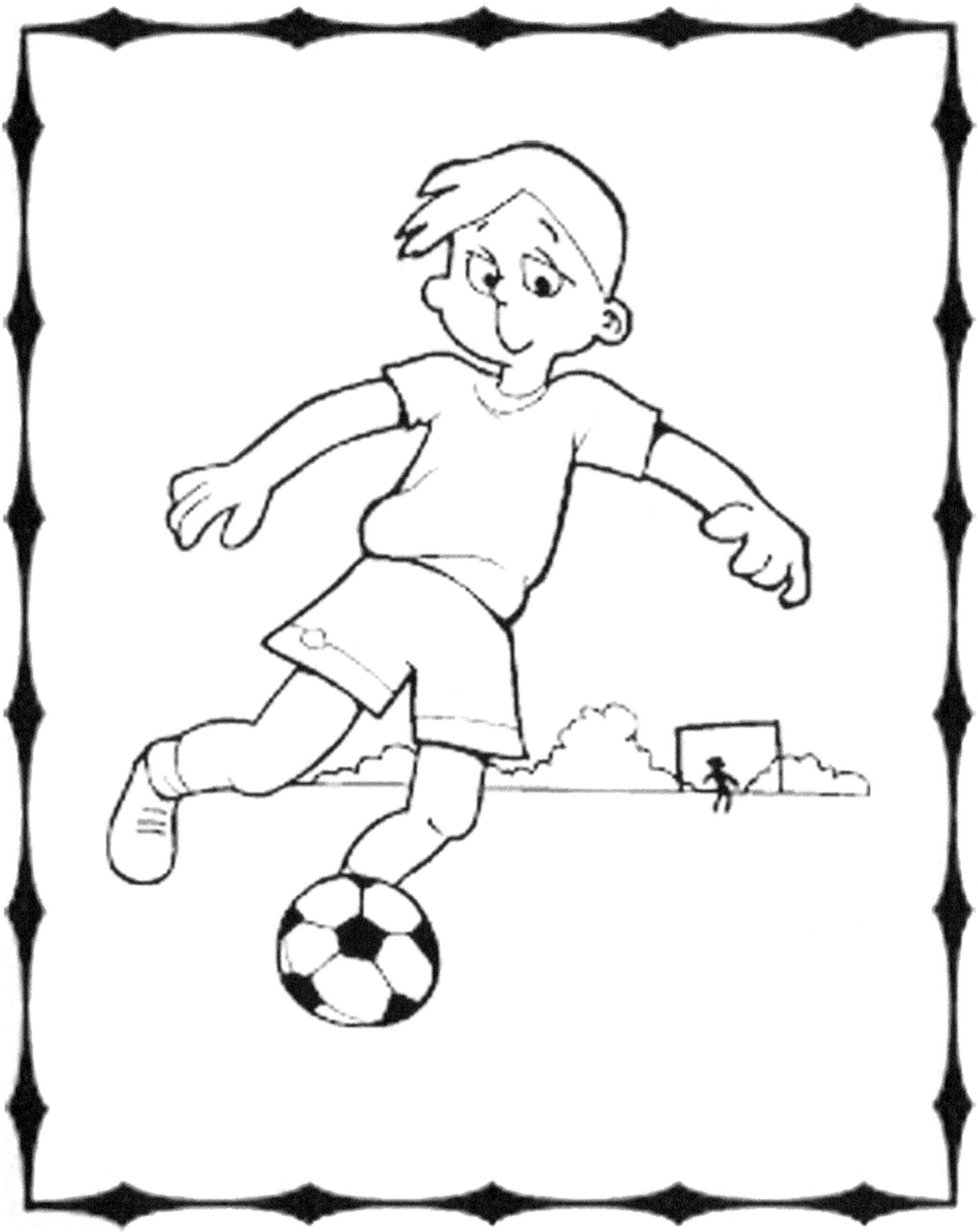

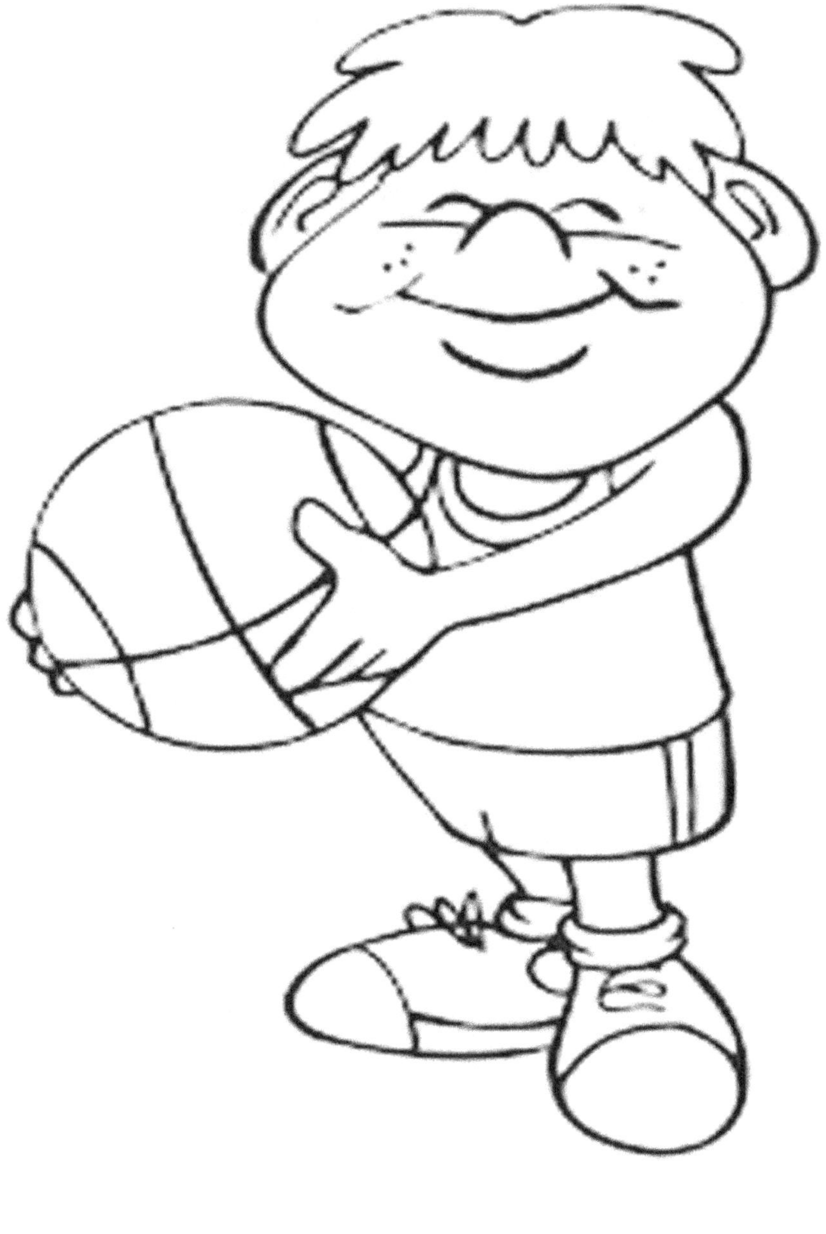

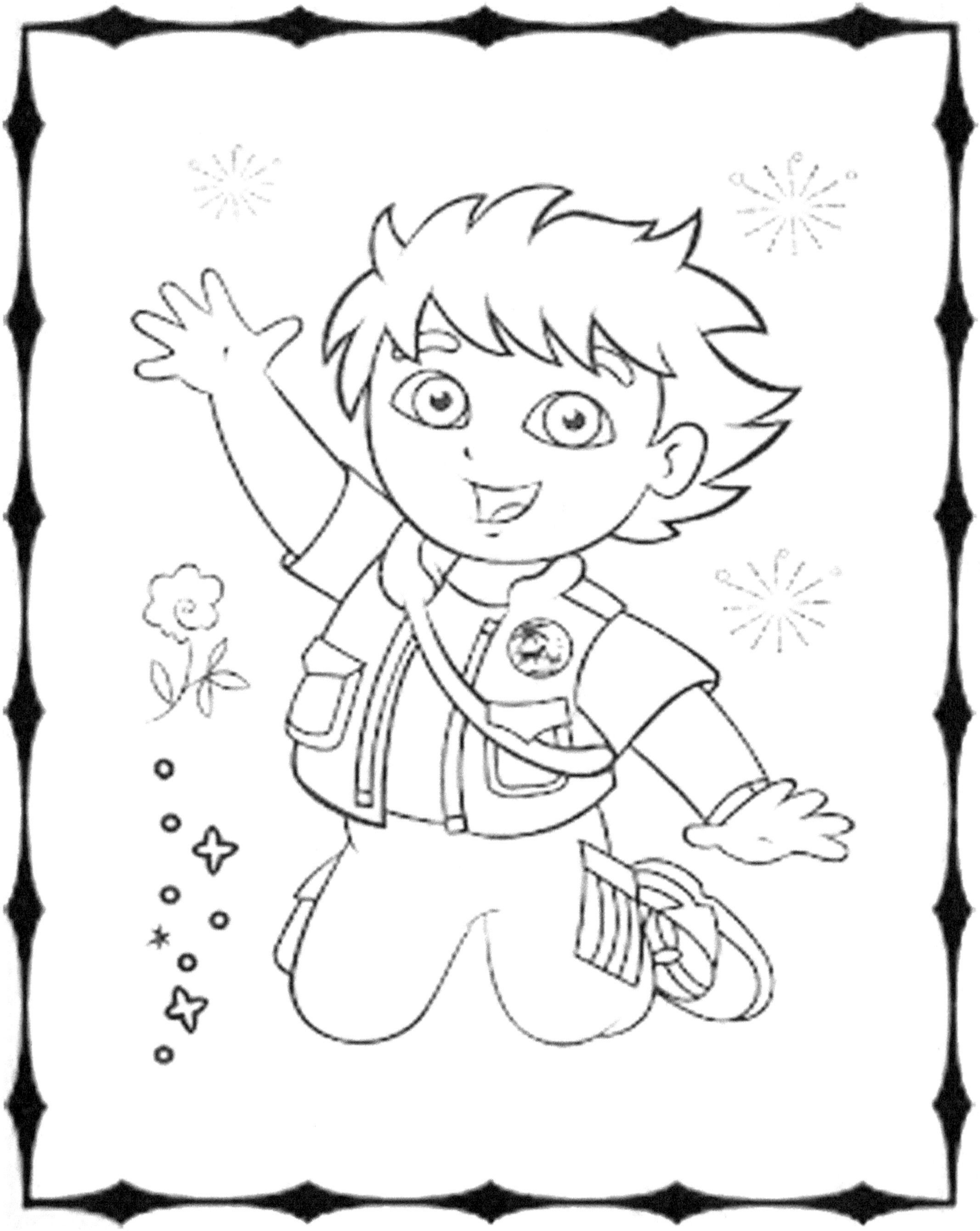

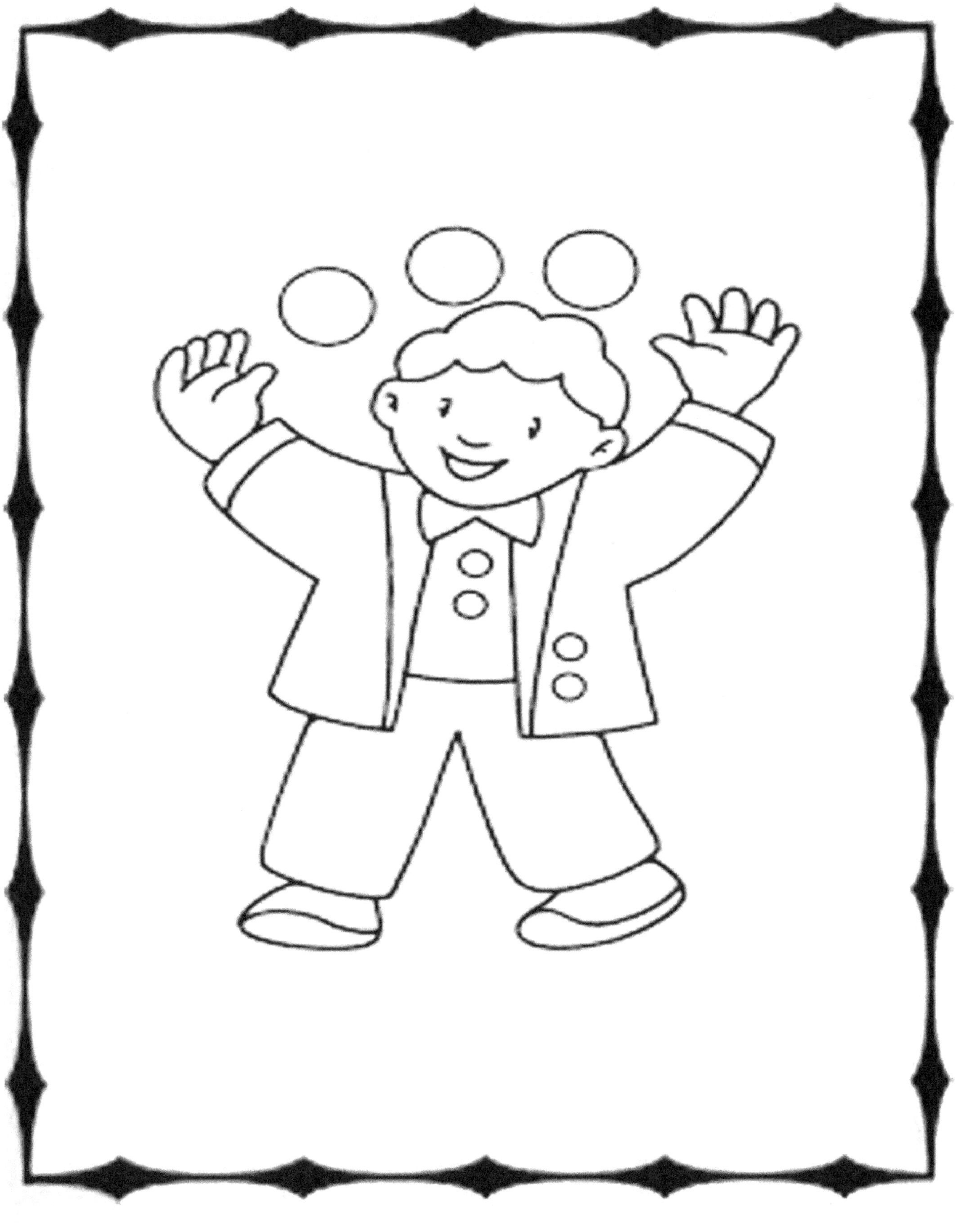

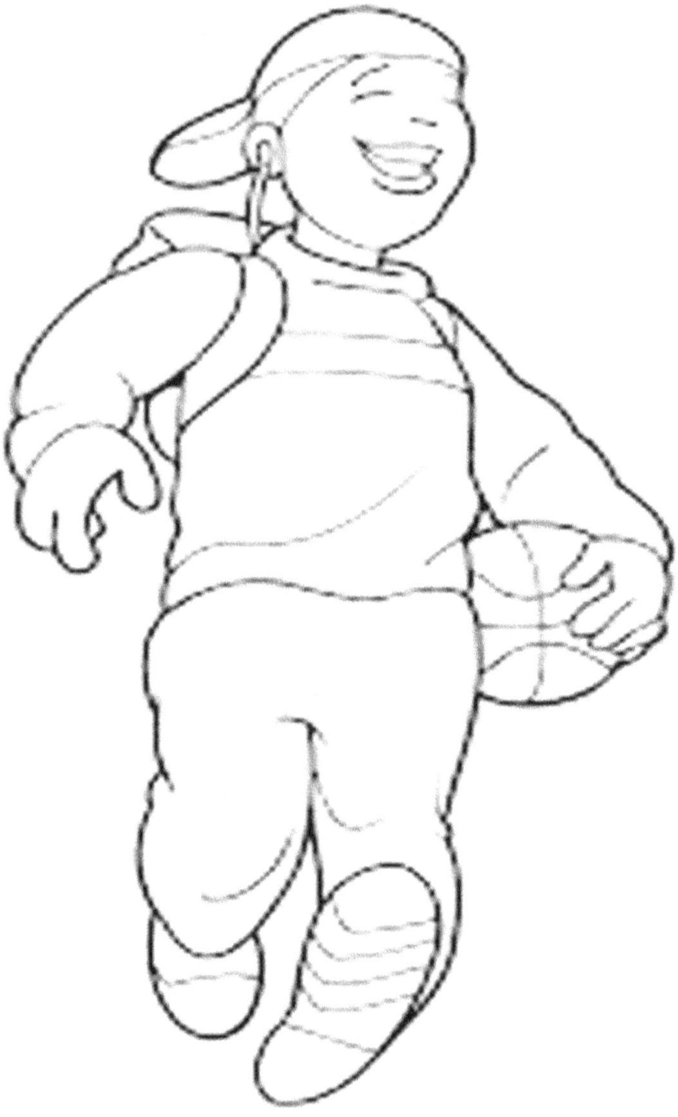

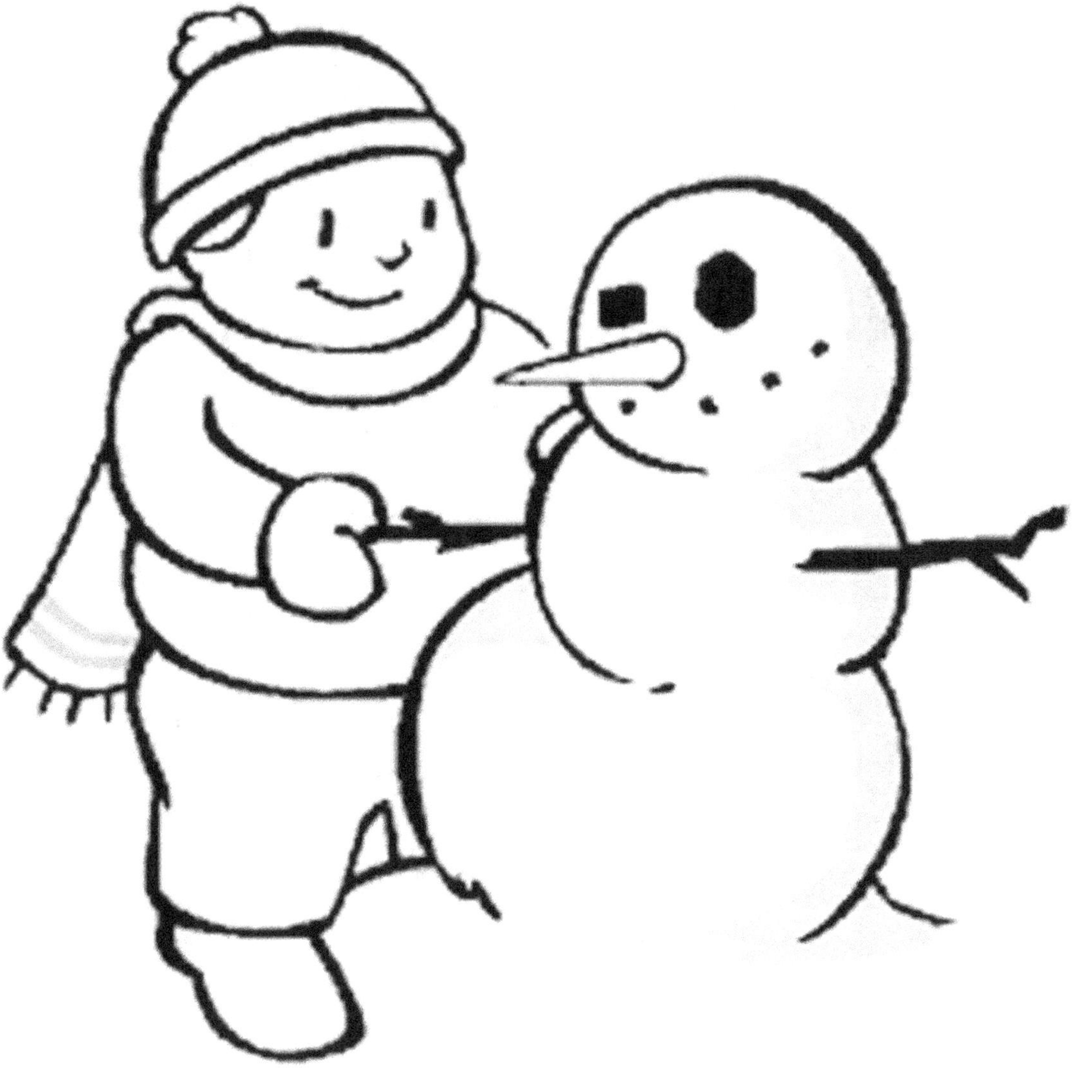

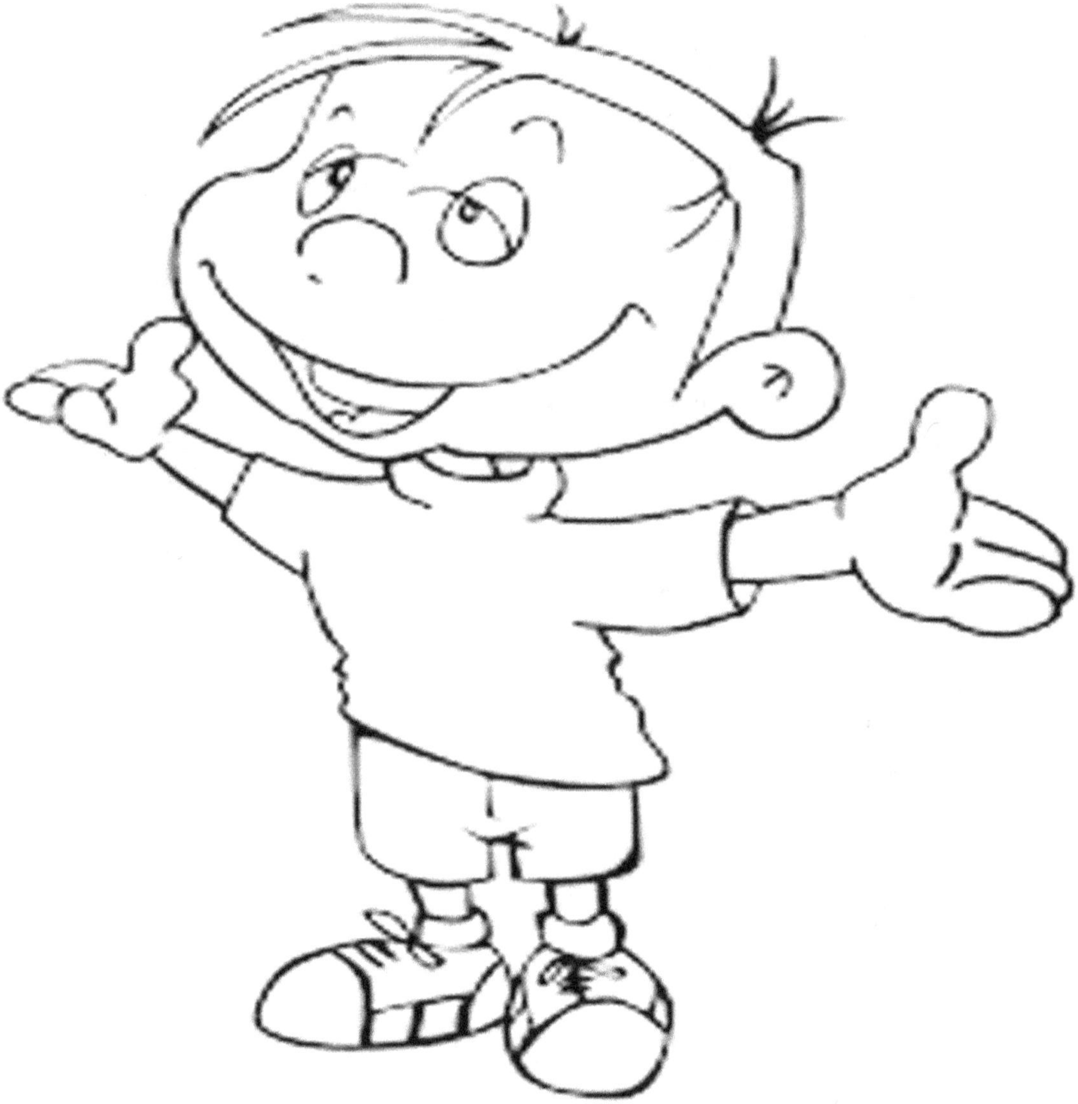

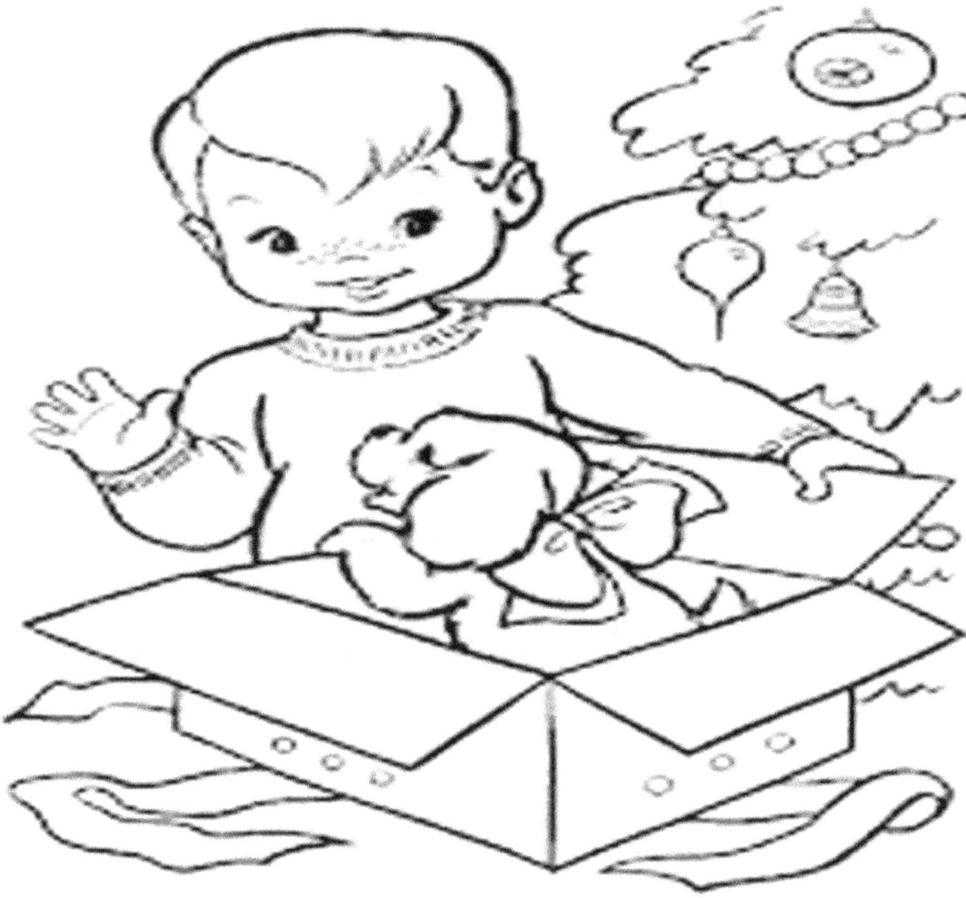

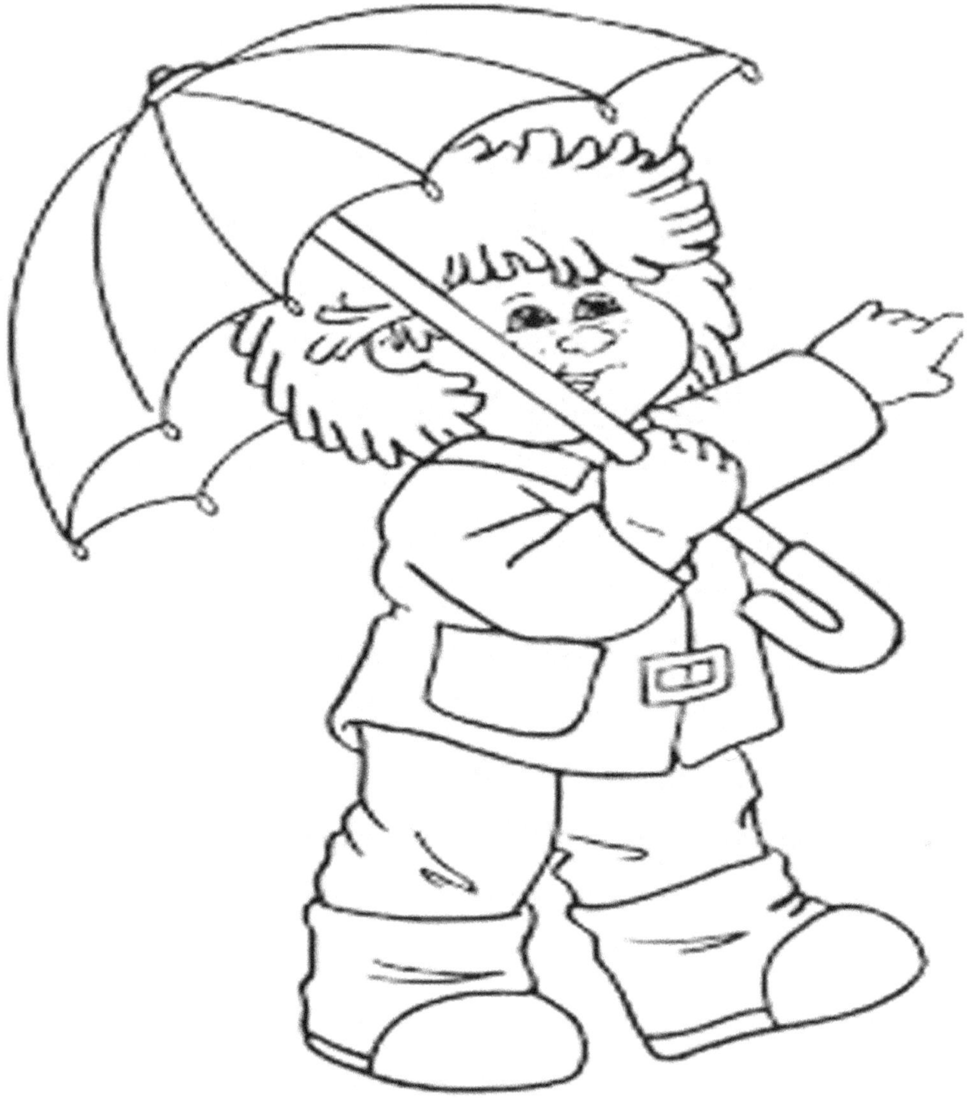

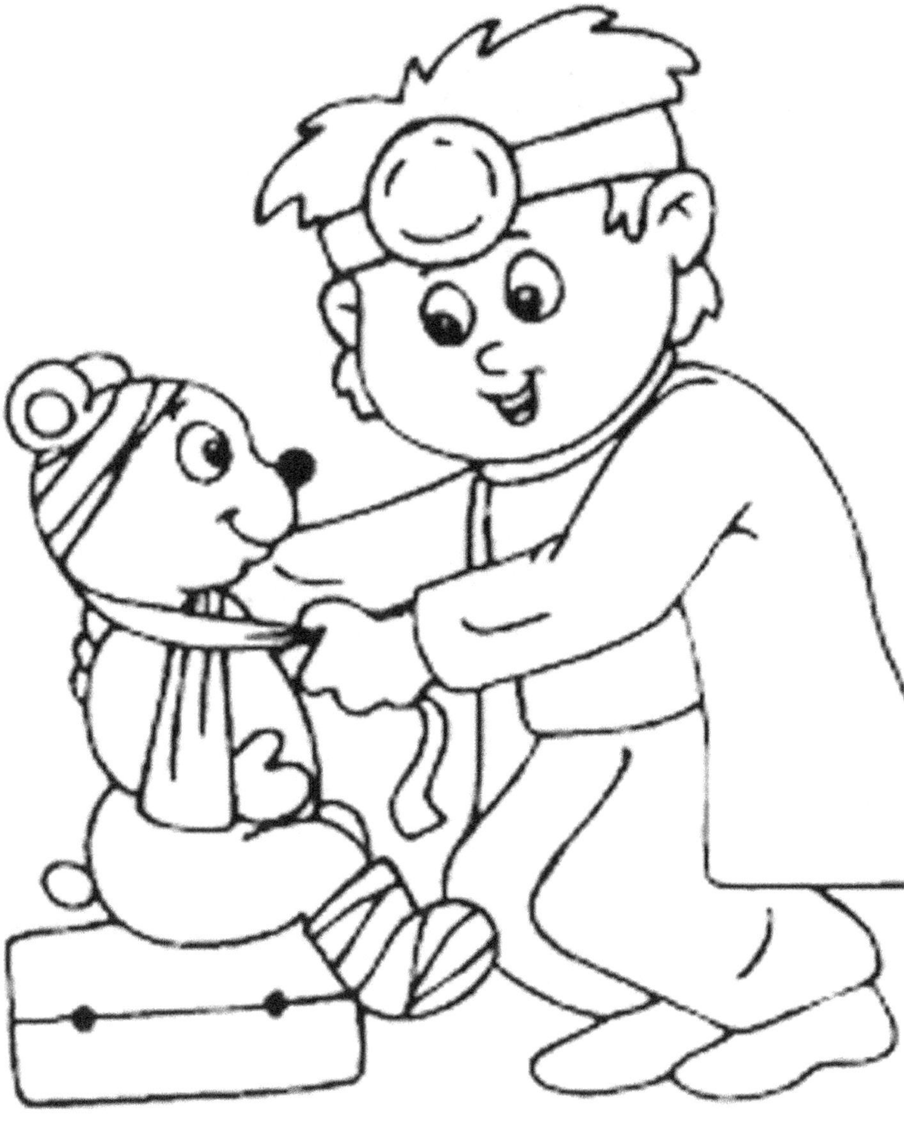

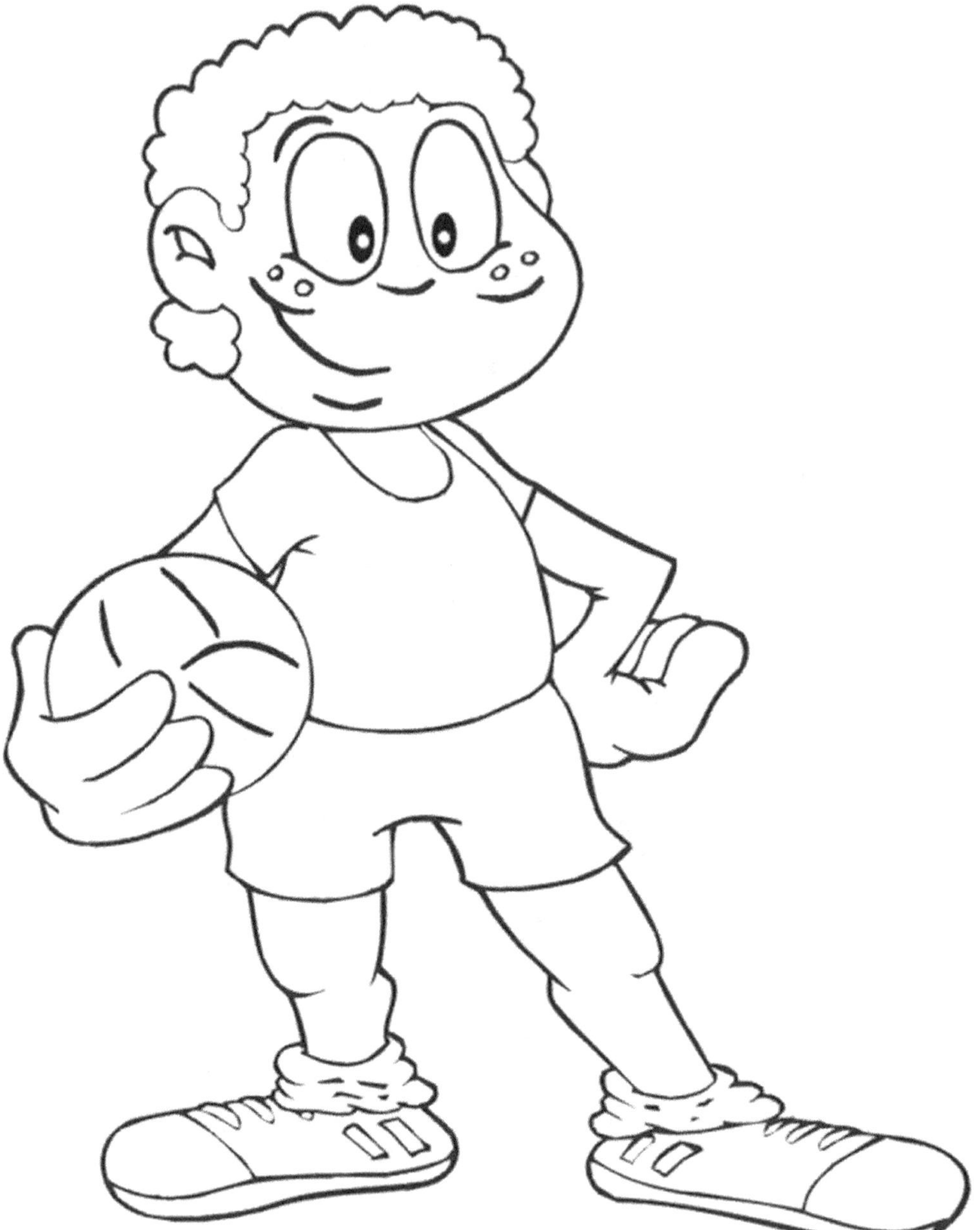

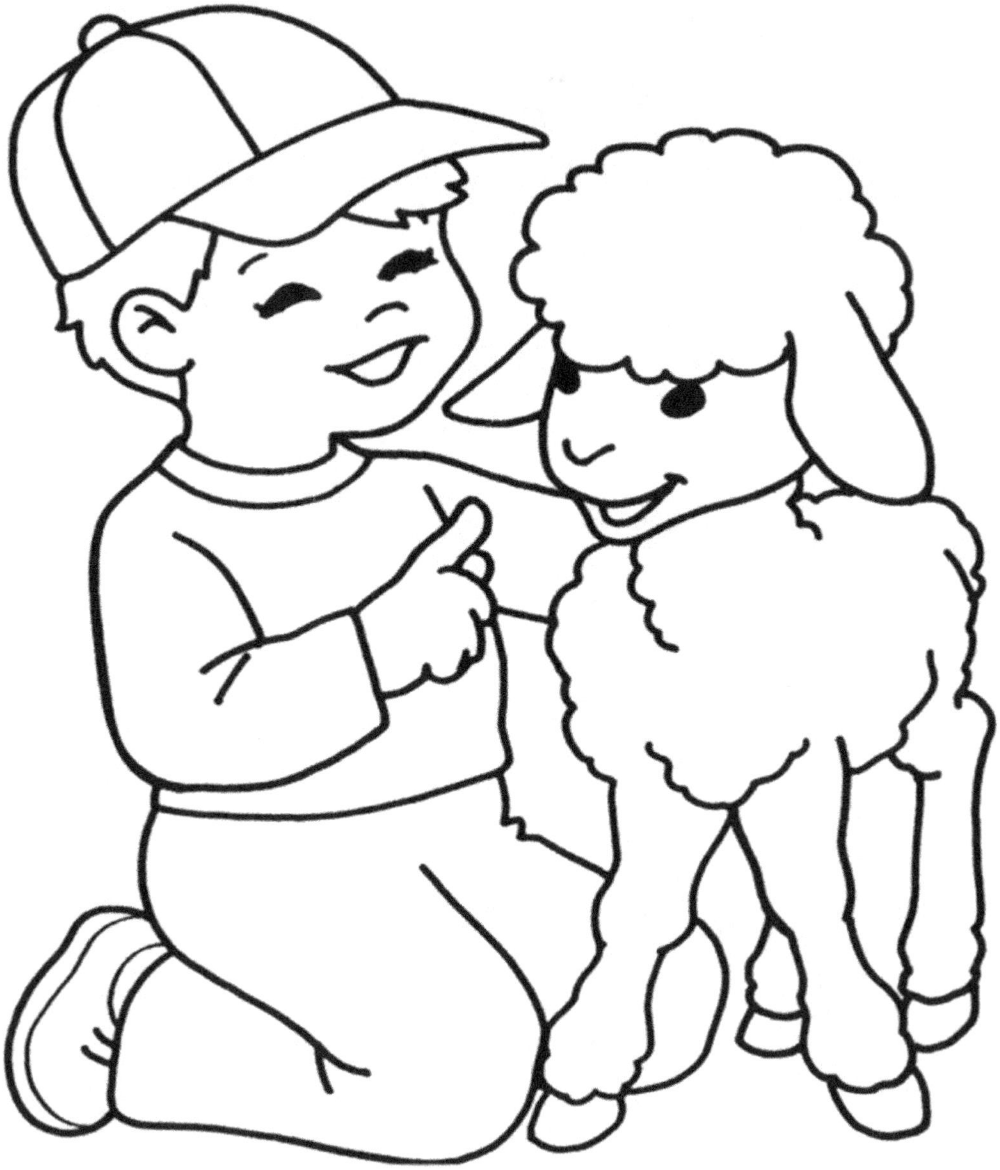

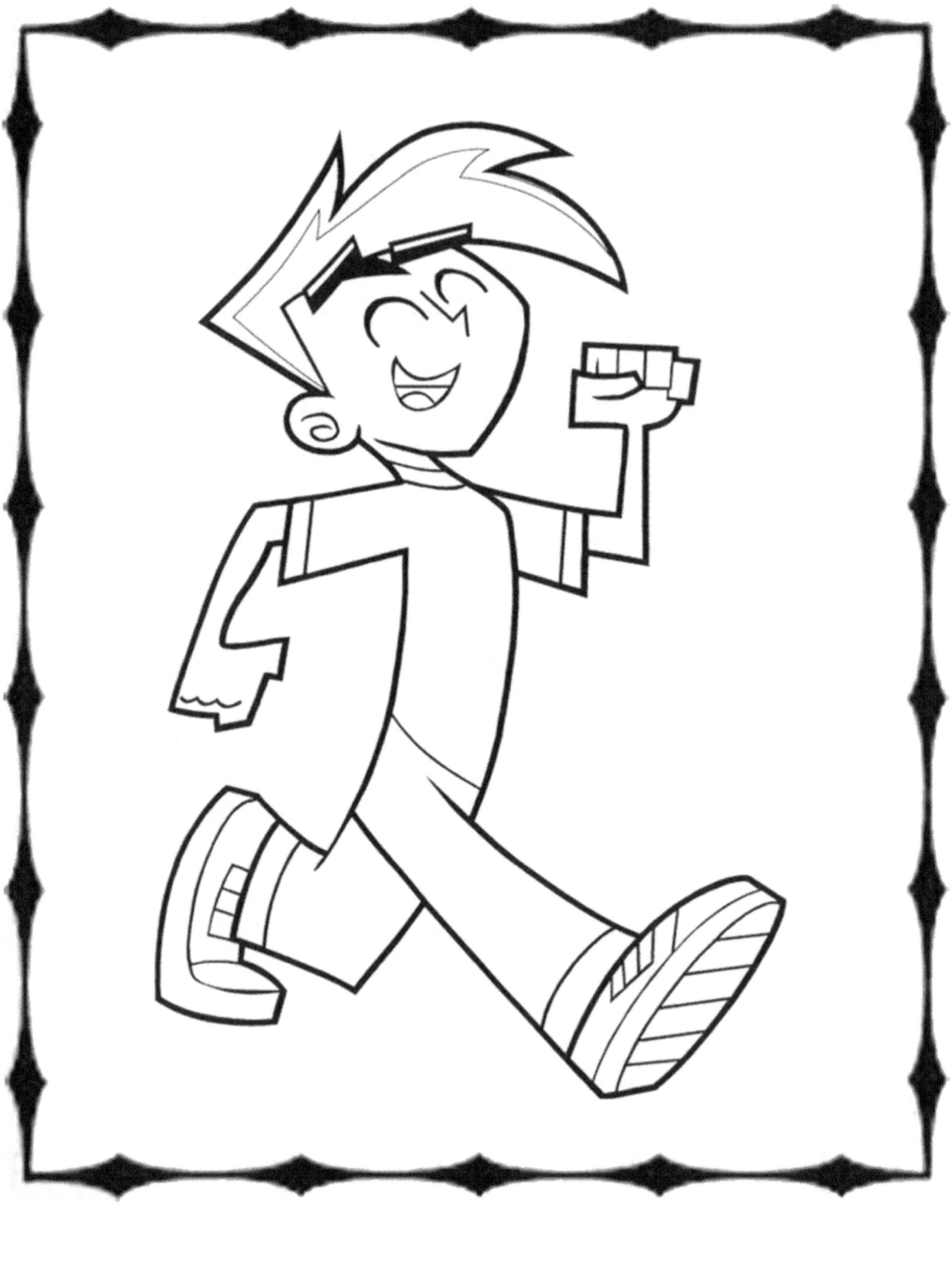

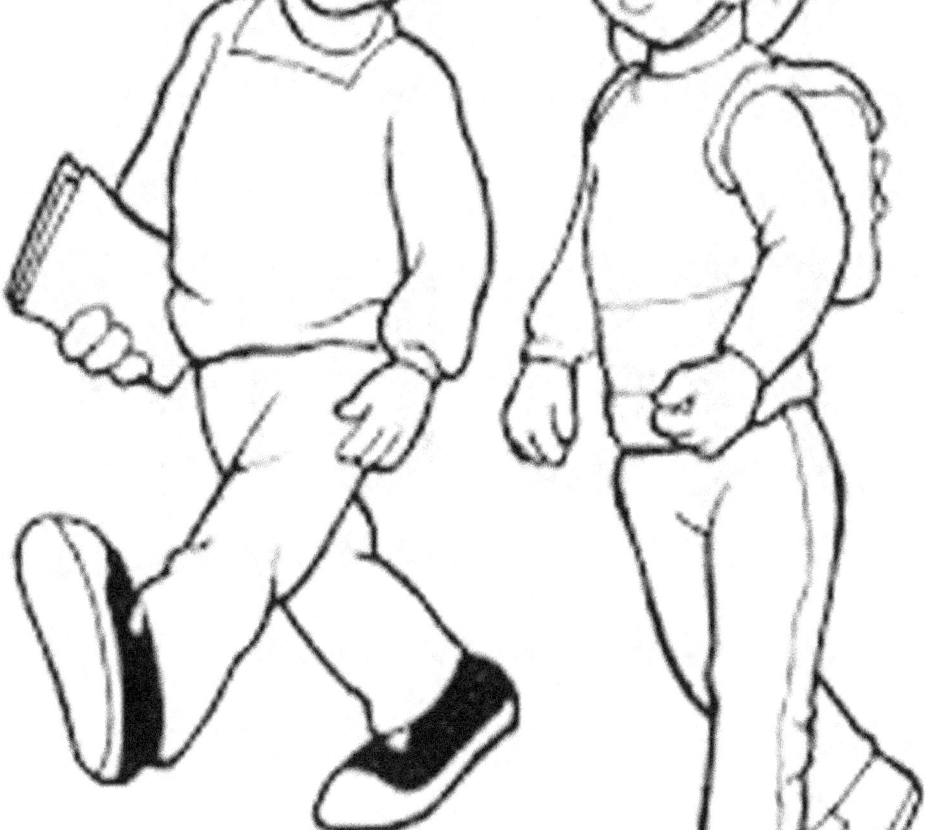

THE END

www.ingramcontent.com/pod-product-compliance
Lightning Source LLC
Chambersburg PA
CBHW082304200526
45168CB00017B/3063
9781508815884